Romantic Riddles

Also by American Poet

John Everett Button

Reflexive Conversations

𝔇(𝔵)⊕

Romantic Riddles

John Everett Button

M&W
PUBLISHING
Milton Chadwick & Waters Publishing
www.MiltonChadwickandWaters.com

Copyright

Romantic Riddles

Published by Milton Chadwick & Waters Publishing
5008 Short Grass Lane, Haymarket, VA 20169
www.MiltonChadwickandWaters.com

Library of Congress Control Number: 2013906759

ISBN : 978-0-9884542-0-0
ASIN: B009164UHS

First Edition

Dedication

"
To her whose state is such that cannot choose

But bend and choose where she is sure to lose

That seeks not to find that her search implies

But, riddle-like, lives sweetly where she dies!
"

~ **William Shakespeare**, *All's Well That Ends Well* (I, iii)

Contents

Illustrations

Preface

*R*omantic *Riddles* is an exploration of one of the most difficult human experiences: love. To genuinely love another person, and be loved in return, is not only supremely difficult, but necessary to the development of a unified personal identity. Love is a prerequisite to a complete understanding of who we are. With each brave attempt to discover love, we find growing within us all the feelings of the laboring mother whose tears of pain and joy become indistinguishable as she gives birth to her child. It is this necessary laboring of the heart that makes love so difficult. The stakes are always high. One must wager everything to discover if their treasure lies in the other person or not. It is all or nothing. They either find themselves perfected in the other, or alone in the growing distance between them.

Romantic Riddles is the result of my heart's boundless resolve to understand the love that I have both gained and lost throughout my life. Consequently, many people have contributed to this book unknowingly and I should like to thank them, in some perverse way, for releasing me back to myself. For in losing the balancing strength of their heart, the immense gravity of my heart pulled upon me and I slowly withdrew into myself. It was in this experience of withdrawing that I took my first step into the quiet temple of solitude that exists alone within me. Solitude, I have come to learn, is as important to self-discovery as relationships are. Throughout the duration of our lives, when love is lost, solitude waits within all of us like a friendly mirror, waiting patiently for us to turn and face ourselves. Through self-reflection, you begin the renewal of the spirit. It's the licking of the wound; the restful sleep after a painful surgery; the slow filling of the lungs after the overwhelming embrace of another. Solitude, like love, is difficult. One must be strong; bear the loneliness that lies beside you at night; endure the strange freedom that you fall through; embrace the emptiness that surrounds you. It is in this movement of the self that one can be nourished and relearn their unique essence, just like an adult relearning the long division of their youth. This book owes its existence to the beautiful suffering of self-discovery I've been forced to endure. Paradoxically, it was in these periods of self-discovery, while others fell farther away, that I have grown closer to that future person whom I will see the perfection of myself in.

Poems don't appear out of a void. The poems in *Romantic Riddles* are no exception. Most of the short poems of part I, "The Love Dialectic" were written in real-time. Like the photographer capturing a bolt of lightning, I captured each poetic image with my pen as it flashed through my heart. Part I provides the reader with pictures of love as it moves between two people. Both dark and light, I hope to give the reader an intimate glimpse behind the curtain of the heart. "Riddles of the Heart" is the second part of Romantic Riddles. Part II displays longer poetic parables about love. The seeds of these poetic parables, or "riddles of the heart" as I have come to call them, became implanted in my heart each time I consumed the ripened fruits of love. Each seed, sufficiently watered by the tears of loss, burst through my heart, blooming into a garden of strange and extraordinary scenes. These scenes grew and matured into the romantic riddles of this book. I wandered through each vivid detail of the riddles as though it were a reoccurring dream that was unknowingly familiar. I wrote down all that I heard, all that I saw. I have left nothing out. Pour through these pages. Let your heart be the sponge that soaks up each scene, each metaphor. Explore everything you see and hear. Turn over each word and see what lies beneath it. Live in them and they will, in turn, live within you.

Acknowledgements

I have been incredibly fortunate to have had the support of many individuals in writing this book. Without their help and encouragement, it would have been impossible, and I would like to thank them: Kristen Brinegar for her undivided encouragement, patience, and inspiration; Philipp Boos for his beautiful sketches that he drew specifically for the book; Adam Sampedro for his book layout help and Allie Franconeri for her beautiful formatting of the book and book layout; Julius Broqueza for his marvelous job in finalizing the book layout and formatting; Brian Zuckerman of cyrenicdesign.com for his beautiful work on the front cover; Aubree Lundie for her thoughtful feedback on earlier drafts; and my photographer Eduardo Rodriguez for his creativity, skill, experience, and time in developing my portfolio and producing my best shoots.

General Introduction

I.

Romantic Riddles

R *omantic Riddles* is a collection of poems that examines the essence of love and the questions, puzzles, and uncertainties that accompany each kiss, intimate encounter, and relationship we experience in our lives. Each poem is infused with some aspect of the heart's greatest puzzle: Love. My original intention was to be a scribe of the human heart – if the heart could speak, what would it say? However, in asking that very question, I could not have anticipated the experience that followed. An entire world overcame me. Scenes of unfathomable circumstances consumed me. I quickly discovered that the heart speaks in riddles that are impossible to comprehend from far away. To understand one, you must step onto the riddle's tender terrain, observe its context, and *feel* the riddle's origin within you. It would be impossible to merely *listen*; one must *live* the riddle. At first, one will find themselves standing at the riddle's end, as though it were a finish line, attempting to gather answers in the riddle's conclusion. The riddle's end is *your* beginning, for one must retrace their steps and *relive* the journey that has brought them there. In reliving it, you will discover, perhaps shockingly, that riddles of the heart do not exist to be answered. They exist to be understood in terms of their origin within you. What painful event planted itself inside the fertile soil of your heart? What caused this vivid emotion to break through its surface and bloom into the fantastic thing within you? Through this discovery process one's attention will shift away from answer seeking to origin seeking. Paradoxically, in this gradual shifting of focus, the distant light of an answer will rise, like a new day, upon the riddle's darkened terrain and you will see the resolution that was always before you: Love. Love is always the question, and love is always the answer. It will always be the cause of the romantic riddle and it will always be its resolution. In the garden of our heart, love is the rose of pure contradiction. Love is life's riddle.

II.

Dividing up the Heart

Romantic Riddles is divided into two parts: "The Love Dialectic," which describes the movement of love between two people and "Riddles of the Heart," which are poetic parables about love itself. "The Love Dialectic," describes and demonstrates the natural movement of love between two people through short vivid poems. These short poems are meant to introduce the reader to my conception of love and the dialectic that produces it. My goal in part I was to *capture* the movement of love through the human heart as it happened. Part I also provides a conceptual foundation of love upon which the entire book is built, enriching one's reading of part II.

The second half of *Romantic Riddles* is found in part II, "Riddles of the Heart." These poems are the main thrust of *Romantic Riddles*. Like a poetic alchemy, these poems combined poem and parable, telling a story that begs some unnamed question. Insofar as part I is a poetic description of the movement of love itself, part II is a clear but frightening abstraction of this concept. These poems challenge the reader's expectations and force a deeper reflection of their own heart. Ultimately, the poems of part II stand in stark contrast to those in part I. By dividing *Romantic Riddles* into two parts, I hope to break-down this riddle of love, and provide a dialectical contrast from which a greater understanding arises.

Part I

The Love Dialectic
(The Movement of Love)

Introduction

The Love Dialectic: The Movement of Love

*T*he love dialectic is the method by which love is conceived between two people; that is to say, love is the result of this unique dialectical process. When two individuals are attracted to one another, they first see themselves as two distinct people. But as time proceeds, and their feelings grow stronger for the other, this distinction of two separate people begins to dissolve. Soon, when they gaze into each others eyes, they do not see a separate person, but rather themselves. As this mutual reflection takes place, they share a unique union of perception as though they were a single entity. It is in this moment that they both transcend their natural born solitude and share a common space and time as one. True love between two people is the transcendence of a single spirit, united from two individuals who see themselves in the other. It is of central importance to human life because it is the only way to experience a full transcendence from the natural-born limitations of our solitude. It is these limitations dictated by our natural solitude that I call the "Riddle of Other Minds."

The Riddle of Other Minds

What could be more certain, more absolute in the eyes of the living, than the experiences that make up their existence? The taste, colors, and smells that we encounter induce the belief of exactly those things we are experiencing. The beauty of our world is forced upon each of us individually. Each individual's experience is private and unique. We are all trapped inside the dark theater of our mind, alone and watching our experiences projected onto the screen before us. We are alone. And so existence goes: we are born alone, confined to our own theater, sitting opposed and independent of what is projected on the screen. It is this *necessary* relation between the individual viewer and what is projected on their screen – this opposition between the beholder and that which is beheld – that defines our perception. But if this is true, then how do we experience ourselves? We may sit in our empty theater opposite the screen, independent of projections before us, but we are not independent of ourselves. How do we step outside of our own theaters to see our own individual beauty? If beauty exists in the eyes of the beholder, how does the beholder behold their own beauty? This question leads us into the riddle of other minds. Stated differently, if beauty is in the eye of an independent beholder, how does the beholder behold their own beauty?

In order to fully view ourselves, we need access to the conscious opposition of ourselves in another living thing. We can imitate this opposition by standing before a mirror, but a mirror provides only the illusion of meaningful opposition; it merely gives us back our own perception of ourselves, nothing more. Nothing new is gained. The mirror may provide some cursory experience of ourselves, but the fact remains that we are tied to the image before us and lack that necessary independent quality (from ourselves) to behold ourselves. Again, the *conscious opposition*, that is, ourselves as seen through the eyes of another being, cannot be achieved through mere self-reflection.

Perhaps, we think to ourselves, we can to sneak into another's theater of experience and see how the world looks through another's eyes, but we try in vain. Our own theater doors are locked. We can't seem to leave our own mind, let alone sneak into another's. So, we resort to communication. We call over the subjective walls of our theaters and speak to one another. We write notes and throw them over, and receive the same in return. But in all this effort, we quickly realize that the experiences we communicate brings us no closer to ourselves (or to others for that matter,) for it is only from our personal reels of perception that we can draw from to understand the notes and messages from others. The riddle of other minds remains unsolved.

Given our natural limitations to gain access into another's theater of the mind, we must try to find our reflection in our beholder; that person who sees our beauty and whom we behold. For two people to behold each other, sitting alone in their theater, seeing the other on the screen, a transformation takes place within both beholders. This transformation is similar to the transformation that takes place when one identifies with a character in a film or play. Eventually the character is seen as a living duplicate of ourselves and not just as representing us. This transformation between two beholders differs because it is reciprocal. For in this reciprocal gaze they first see the beauty of the other. As their gaze continues, feelings develop for the other, and they begin reciprocating each others interest and experiences. Then, as their feelings mature, an image of themselves emerges in the other, like a reflection or living duplicate of themselves. This self-realizing whittles away at the distinctions between the beholder and that which is beheld until these distinctions collapse and vanish. And although they remain alone inside their own theaters of perception, they feel as if they have scaled the subjective walls of their theaters, transcended their own borders, and experience the world together as two lovers, huddled together in a darkened theater, watching their favorite movie.

Romantic
Riddles

Love Dialectic

When I see you, *time* plunges into me,
flooding the ceased movement of my heart.

In that *moment*, a sudden chill rushes up my neck
and my reflection appears before me,
rooting itself in my mind
like a picture inside a frame.

The Object of Life

After George Gordon Byron

The object of life is sensation; to *feel* that we exist –

touch me, my love,
kiss me,
press your body against mine –

give me knowledge of my existence.

The Hour-glass Between Us

Time falls inside the gaze we share
like sand inside an hour-glass,
where nothing, not even our love, can stop the time
that settles in the space between us.

Vanishing Act

The moment she looks at me,
My mind empties of all the experiences that collect,
Like gentle rain, into my eyes

The moment she touches me
My body vanishes, leaving only my soul before her like a
lingering smoke,

Which she inhales, pulling me
Inside of her where the warmth of her love can best be felt

When her heart is satisfied, she exhales me with her sigh
And I reappear

Cease to Exist

As day disappears
Releasing the dark light of night
You close the bedroom door behind you;
Only we exist
In the candle light

As you approach me
The sounds of the city become distant;
As your hands and knees press into the bed,
The world falls out from beneath us
Only we exist tonight

And when our lips touch
We have lost our names, ourselves
And have only this moment left
As we close our eyes
And disappear from sight

Telekinesis

The eyes have power: Watch her carefully or she may vanish

at any moment.

When she looks up

You will find yourself walking towards her

As though possessed with sudden abandon

Of yourself –

no past,
no future,
only now.

When she turns towards you,
Both of you will close your eyes
As she kisses you

Love is a Language
Spoken in Heated Silence

Like some first human,
pretend that language was impossible
and indistinct utterances are all that can be heard

Like two strangers who meet in the dark,
let's touch what we have not yet seen
and fulfill our imaginations

Like a secret you've never shared
hold me closely
between your legs

Smother me with your desire:
Make me push your hair from my face
and keep your lips upon me

Kiss me with urgency
and let your body speak to me
as though no wish would go unfulfilled

Let your eyes call out to me
when you can no longer breathe
and thought becomes impossible

Binary Stars

I follow you, but you do not lead me
You follow me, but I do not lead you

We share the same space,
but never at the same time
We are never apart, but never together

How do we manage such a union?

We are like two stars,
circling each other forever and ever

To Love from a Distance

Tonight,
we watch the same

  moon

  Linger in the night sky like a
    comet

  frozen in a crescent
    flame

  And just as it silently gazes down upon both of us
I too, gaze down upon you
          in my heart

Dream of a Dream of Me

Close your eyes and spy upon yourself
        See the dreams that you dream
        Hear the song that your heart sings
        while you sleep

Dream a dream of me
        Look at me and see yourself
                Know your heart as I do
        Carry me up the steep slopes of your mind
        to the crest of your sky

                        Show me the world from your height

Fireworks

Look, my beloved!
Our love shoots into the night sky,
twirling towards the divine reality of an ideal.

Still higher it climbs!
Our love thrills upward into our secret sky,
slowing around the curves and bendings of pleasure.

It has burst!
A constellation blooms before our eyes,
eternal in our gaze as it fades from the sky.

Romantic Riddles

Your words are roses
    riddled with unseen thorns,
snagging my tender heart,
    leaving it tattered and torn.

Each beat of my heart
keeps it from mending
    because my love won't rest
    This end is unending

Boots 2012

Part II

Riddles of the Heart

Introduction

Riddles of the Heart

*T*he poems contained in "Riddles of the Heart" are
the main thrust of *Romantic Riddles*. They are a poetic
alchemy, combining poem and parable, to give a
glimpse behind the heavy curtain of the heart. Insofar as "The
Love Dialectic" describes different aspects on the movement
of love, the poetic parables of "Riddles of the Heart" are an
extraordinarily frightening abstraction of this concept. Each
poem conjures up vast, awe-inspiring worlds that exist in a
seemingly timeless terrain. The affairs of the heart detailed
in each poetic parable run the full range of emotions, from
joyous fulfillment to startling despair. As in real life, solutions
are absent and some events go on unexplained. These poems
challenge the reader's expectations and force a deeper reflection
of themselves and those that they loved in their life.

Romantic
Riddles

When is a Rose not a Rose?

The old mountain felt the footsteps of the young couple upon his rounded back,
hiking up his warn path, searching for his overlook at the top.
The autumn wind ran her fingers through the tops of his tall trees,
combing crippled leaves from his branches, covering his trails with debris.

The old mountain heard the girl's timid steps upon the crisp leaves
as she followed closely behind her young lover,
looking down, careful to avoid large roots and rocks,
quietly wondering where her lover was taking her.

The old mountain calmed the busy autumn and listened with tenderness
as the young girl took a deep breath
and asked: "Do you love me?"
The boy continued forward, looking up ahead for the overlook,

"Yes."
She looked up without certainty, wondering why
a rock shifted beneath her foot, forcing her attention
back upon the old path.

The young couple neared the top of the old mountain's trail,
walking through the woods to the open mouth of the overlook.
Together they stood upon the lip of the white rocks that jetted down
the mountain's face like a long white beard.

She immediately felt the distance of all things, as if her eyes reached out,
grasping at the broad-winged hawk that soared away from the mountain
and over the village in the valley far below.
The boy saw this and placed a rose, hidden in his jacket, into her hand.

She smiled upon the rose and asked slowly, "Why do you love me?"
His gaze fell into the bare branches of the trees far below
and after a moment of deliberation, looked upon the rose in her hand and asked:
"Should I have given you the rose's roots as well?"

Thoughts of You

"Don't you know you can see me…the one you love in the water"
~ Juliet, *L'ATALANTE* (1934)

Thoughts of you arise like new day,
bleaching my mind in bright light,
awakening me beneath a moving sky.

I find myself cradled in a boat
in the middle of a windless sea,
wondering where you may be.

Peering over the boat's edge,
and into my muddled reflection,
I begin to find you

gently wavering below the surface.

As you look into my eyes, the world falls away, leaving only you before
me, radiating warm moving light that softly presses against me.
Turning slightly and holding your arm across your breast, I see all of you.

You smile and reach out to me.

But as I extend my hand, your warm light recedes
into the dark emerging sea that holds you again.
You begin to fade into the darkening water.

The evening sky begins to wither apart and fall,
exposing the open night. Soon glowing ashes are upon me,
falling slowly like burning snow, dissolving into the still sea.

As I reach into the water for you
my hand scatters my reflection
and you are gone.

On Her 18th Birthday

They sat beside each other in silence
watching the waves crash along the beach,
just as they had always wanted to.

It was her 18th birthday and her father took her to the beach;
the one place they both loved;
the one place he could never make time for.

The first half of the day, they walked along the old pier
that groaned like an old wooden ship that laid upon the shore,
gently swaying with the waters that rushed beneath it.

From the piers edge, they looked out upon the vast sea that rolled
towards them. He talked of his father taking him there as a kid. He said
being a son and only child, he was lucky to have that time with him.

He said her grandfather would stand at the pier's edge with him
and ask him, "If this was a ship, where would you want to go?"
When he didn't have an answer he was told,

"You *must* go somewhere, son. That's what a ship is built for!"
After a short pause, he told her that he felt like he was the old pier
finally being pushed out to sea.

They passed beneath the seagulls scattered above the shore,
wings outstretched, suspended in flight with the warm western winds
that swept along the beach.

He had spent the afternoon talking to her about trust,
retelling the story of her mother going away
and how much he still loved her.

He reminded her of how proud he was of her
for raising her younger brother and taking care of the house
during the day, since he had to work long shifts at night.

He said that he didn't regret having a daughter,
even knowing that he would have to leave her when she turned 18,
never to see or communicate with her again.

He said the community's custom *just is* – just like the ocean before
them. The ocean was a fact of life, with its tide churning away the
shore each year swallowing *his* beach; his time; his memories.

As much as he didn't want to leave that night, he had to follow custom
and give away his daughter; give her to herself,
so she could freely give her love to another man the next day.

As they sat on the beach, he began to tell her how much he loved her, pausing
as his eyes would redden, welling up with water, before he clenched his
jaw, and slowly exhaled. She had never heard him express himself before.

Her head cleared suddenly and, for an instant, she found the custom impossible.
She looked back and saw how far they were from the community
and wondered if they could just leave together;

leave the house to her brother; leave her job; leave the community.
She saw herself writing to her mother, telling her about the move with her dad
and that she should come and live with them.

But her thoughts were interrupted by the motion of her father's wrist.
He looked at his watch and back towards the darkening sky.
She knew their time was almost up.

As the wind died down, she said with forced indifference,
"Maybe we can just go find our own beach and live there."
"I don't think so sweetheart. The same ocean would be there too."

The sun had vanished into the ocean.
She felt the darkened waters of the tide climbing closer to their feet.
"Maybe we can come back another time and do this…"

His eyes reddened and he turned his head away. His neck trembled.
With a shallow breath, he said with an exaggerated southern draw,
"Ah, I *would* if I *could* Kris. You know how these things go."

Feeling the cold shock of the tide upon her toes,
the vivid possibilities quickly receded from her memory.
"Yeah, I guess you're right, dad."

If Love were an Army

From the towering walls that encircle your heart, you watch legions of solders,
Stretching back as far as the eye can see, steadily marching forward
With polished golden helmets and body armor gleaming in the high-noon sun.
The legions are flanked by tall archers in loose white garments:
Long golden bows strung over their shoulders; dark leather wraps their forearms;
Thin silver arrows rest in furry quivers across their backs.
By the thousands they surge forward;
A glittering tide of gold flooding the open field.

In the distant wake of the infantry and archers emerge a single line of cavalry:
Powerful black horses carrying riders, dressed in bright silver armor, stretched
Across the entire field, long black mohawk-crests soar down the middle of their silver
helmets; loose silver flaps hang down from the side of their helmets, framing their
shadowed faces. Following behind this dark wall of horses is a golden chariot
Its muscular driver, wearing only a pleated leather kilt, holds in his right hand
The reigns to three long-haired white horses, stiffly prancing forward
With each thunderous crack of his golden whip.

This magnificent chariot led an imperial train:
Priests, in long white robes with embroidered golden patterns, chant in monotone voices;
Young flower girls, with wooden hand baskets, toss purple flower pedals into the air;
Trumpeters, with large flaring bronze bells that circle over their shoulder and head,
Sounded a golden-framed lectica, with four dark-wooden posts resting on the bare
Shoulders of servants. At the end of the procession, draped in fine velvet cloth and studded
In amethyst stones. The decadent carriage hovers over the path of purple flower pedals
And is placed down upon the ground.

The trumpeters call out, from their great distance, to the front lines.
A sudden silence of feet passes over the field.
You feel as though your walls have already been breached
By an army of eyes, so focused on you, that they are unaware of each other.
The tall archers, now within bowshot, pull long silver arrows from their quivers and
Load them onto their golden bows, using their hands and feet to heave the taut bowstrings
back. Turning sideways and leaning slightly back, they raise their bows into the air and
Hold their position.

The trumpets sound a third time. A small messenger
With a long white-haired plume and mounted on a decorated white horse,
Emerges from behind the royal carriage,
Launching himself into the vast sea of golden helmets before him;
The voyage before him is long and daunting.
He slowly navigates through each century
Parting the infantry lines
That close back around him as he passes.

Finally breaking through the front lines with rigid posture and a calm unwavering stare,
He trots towards you with supreme confidence as though he were laying siege to the
Stronghold himself. You've heard stories of this royal herald and his imperial message:
A promise of happiness in exchange for the treasures of your heart.
How you wish you could surrender like so many others before you
And avoid the siege that will follow if you resists.
The messenger approaches the great wall, and calls up to you:

"Have no fear! We do not want to occupy this bastion of the heart, but liberate it!"
        "What is it that you want?"
"We want the same as you."
        "And what is that?"
"You have inscribed riddles of love upon these walls, and now we have come for the an-
swers that are confined inside your heart; answers withheld from you and I. We must open
your heart to retrieve the treasures inside it. Our offer is generous: Surrender and allow us
past your walls, and there will be no battle. Resist and we will breach these walls, no matter
how painful the siege."

He can see, as he has seen before, blankness swoon over your eyes
As you lean heavily upon the wall's edge, looking out
upon the vast sea of golden helmets stretching off into the distance,
unable to reply.
The sun begins to set behind you; casting each soldier's shadow; multiplying the army.
Frozen in their heroic stances, the archers' arrows aim towards the lowered sun
As you gaze upon them, you feel the tension
Of the bowstring held in their two fingers, and grow sick

As they release their arrows into the fiery depths of the evening sky.
Like a cloudless rain, you watch their silent descent with hopelessness.
In this last moment, still unable to reply, your eyes manage to leave the sky
And call out, with all the air left in your lungs, to the imperial messenger
who is speedily galloping away:

"Who is the ruler that hides in that golden-framed carriage?"
The messenger, turning slightly over his shoulder, shouts back

"The golden carriage is empty – it awaits you since this is your army!"

The Dark Passages
of the Heart

The dark passages of his heart hold precious secrets
in the rough, wet walls that have been excavated
by the tireless struggle of her hidden hands.

It is only a matter of time before the pressure
of promises, and the sweltering heat of desire, crystallize
the secrets buried so deep within his heart.

He is certain she expects to find him hiding in a dark corner,
waiting to be found with a handful of precious stones,
ready to confess to all that can be confessed.

But she hasn't. So, she will continue digging,
until his heart collapses,
burying him with all of his secret treasures.

The Garden

(A Poem in 3 Parts)

I.

For her entire youth she sat in her open windowsill combing her long blond hair,
watching day and night gently pass over her, again and again.
How complete she felt as the entire world circled around her.

One day, she looked down and noticed that she had grown considerably.
Sitting cross-legged, the tips of her long blond hair curled into her lap.
She parted her hair down the middle and began braiding the first half.

When she looked up, she was startled to see a garden blooming in the west:
small trees steadily rising over young leafy plants and brightly colored flowers.
Even from her great distance, the garden's colors captured her innocent gaze.

Every morning, she waited eagerly for the garden to emerge from night.
Every evening she watched the sun sink into the hill's growing trees.
Each night she watched a full moon cast its pale shadow upon the garden.

How complete she felt as she held all the colors of the garden
in her dreamy gaze. It was as if by merely looking upon it,
it belonged to her and its purpose was fulfilled. When she finished

braiding the first half of her hair, she noticed the windowsill had become
smaller still. She now had to lean slightly over to fit in its shrinking space.
As she braided the second half of her hair, she looked up, and was stunned:

the garden had grown so high that it consumed the entire western sky;
so full that the sun disappeared entirely during its evening descent;
the moon ascended, like a ghost, from the tops of the trees.

How incomplete she felt as the garden divided her night and day.
She could no longer feel the gentle tug of the moon as it passed over her,
or the warm winds of the sun as it descended into night.

This feeling only worsened with each shorting pass of the sun and moon.
She felt as though she was in a foreign land, far from the world's center.
The garden had become so large; her eyes could no longer hold it.

II.

After a century of sleepless moments waiting for a glimpse of the moon's pale cheeks, she felt as though nothing belonged to her; not even her beautiful hair. That night she felt a gentle stirring of her soul; an innate sense of curiosity

began to flutter from within her chest. Suddenly, she watched her heart fly out of her and migrate, like a butterfly, towards the garden's dark overbearing presence. She knew she had to follow her heart. She finished braiding her hair

and watched the garden bloom in the early morning light. It was now so enormous and colorful that she couldn't look upon it without feeling overwhelmed and lost. She squeezed out of the cramped windowsill

and left her house forever, steadily walking towards the great garden, following her heart. After a lifetime of walking, she stood before the garden and was filled with complete and utter awe:

The trees were huge wooden columns that disappeared into the clouds, swaying in slow circles, stirring the high mists. Entering the garden, she passed entire colonies of white, pink, red, orange, and yellow roses.

She discovered a path that led through the thick undergrowth and followed that path hopeful that it was the path to her heart. The sun followed her overhead, glittering through the dense garden trees and giving light to the darkened path.

When she came to the middle of the garden, she stopped before a tall young man squatting down and planting seeds from a leather satchel slung over his shoulder. He had short dark hair, light-brown eyes, and a beautifully square jaw.

Ignoring her with a slight sigh, he continued his work.
She watched him gently pat the seeds into the tender soil.
Life sprang up from the earth as if by silent command.

Trees popped and whined as they climbed upward. New branches scratched and clawed surrounding trees. He threw handfuls of red and purple seeds around the trees. Roses and violets immediately sprung open.

The sun was still directly overhead, its light entangled in the new trees.
She felt balanced again, for she was in the garden, the new center of the world.
Standing on this new equator, she knew fulfillment was within her grasp.

But in this moment of reflection, she realized how fragile such comfort was,
for her feelings were rooted in the garden's existence –
if a tree should fall or a flower wilt, what then?

Focusing on the handsome young gardener, she marveled
at the power he wielded in the garden with his gentle hands.
The leather pouch was his mind; the seeds were his thoughts.

She slowly chased him, walking behind him, anxiously watching him.
The sun followed overhead like a chaperon as they walked west. With each careful
step, he examined the ground for bare soil to lay his thought down.

They came to the edge of a small bluff at the end of the garden.
Together they looked out over an open world. She saw her heart in everything.
With dazzled eyes, she reached out, but could not seize the beauty she saw:

great flocks of birds flying out towards the sun and moon;
deer standing on the banks of a distant pond, drinking its water;
a fox trotting through tall grass and disappearing into the earth.

She turned towards the handsome gardener who looked out upon all of his cre-
ation, and saw that he held it firmly with the glowing amber of his eyes.
He held her heart in his creation and she now wished to reclaim it.

Breaking the gardener's watchful gaze, she said, *And now I look upon you!*
He turned and looked directly into her eyes, as if to examine her soul,
And said,

III.

*You can have whatever you see; look upon it and it's yours! Your heart now
rest within mine. Just as I look upon myself in your eyes right now, and see
only you, you must find yourself in my eyes and behold my heart. Do this and
we will both be fulfilled!*

She looked up into his eyes, and saw her reflection.
She had never seen herself before and felt overwhelming joy,
as she finally was one with herself.

He smiled, seeing that she had discovered herself in him,
but her gaze was frozen; she could not let go of herself.
Seeing this, as he had seen several times before,

the gardener withdrew himself and turned away,
retreating back into his garden alone,
leaving her in a moment of disbelief.

Her mind became empty of herself. Confidence seeped from her eyes
and streamed down her cheeks. She strained to hold everything
that was before her, but her teary eyes couldn't see anything.

Her whole world began to crumble. The sun shook the ground beneath her feet as it
burst into a thousand pieces upon the land. The clouds it plunged through burned
like cotton torches in the night sky.

The risen moon, shrouded into the fiery-clouds, quickly disintegrated,
leaving a cold silvery mist that fell upon the land
and across the backs of the animals that fled through the tall grass.

The stars slowly fell from their ancient realm,
disappearing behind the darkness of the horizon,
but she saw none of this for her hands covered her weeping eyes.

The Great Wall of Expectation

Being the only maiden in the land, she found with the utmost ease, dissatisfaction with every suitor presented to her. When she dismissed every suitor in the Sultan's land, the rumblings of the rejected could be heard outside her door, demanding she choose a husband. She assured the angry mob they would receive an answer the following afternoon. Once the mob disbanded, she swiftly left her house and, under the cover of the night, passed through the city gates.

As she walked beneath the stars, she gazed into the night sky, seeing her lover in its boundless depths with qualities as bright and numerous as the stars. When she turned and saw the torches of the city's outermost walls extinguish themselves into the desert, she laid down upon the dry flat earth and rested. As her eyes grew heavy, her lover brightened in the sky, emerging as a constellation. With tired eyes, she reached out and held him in her empty grasp, holding him as long as she could remain awake. As she fell asleep, she watched his stars disintegrate and fall, like glitter, down upon her.

A cloud of cologne awoke the princess from a deep sleep. She found herself lying in the shadow of a narrow brick wall that climbed endlessly into a blue sky; its thin shadow stretched across the desert plain, touching the distant mountains on the horizon. She recognized the great wall, for she had dreamt of it the previous night. She could remember a voice hidden within its bricks repeating, over and again, that only her true love could dissolve the great the wall.

As she circled around it, moving into the daylight, she discovered a long line of men, stretching off into the distance, waiting anxiously for her. When she appeared to them their hearts stopped, seized by her beauty. They could no longer see the wall beside her, for they stood in awe of a beauty that was greater than the sum of the wall's parts. They gazed adoringly at her

long black hair, parted down the middle, framing her beautiful face and her large Persian eyes, which were so inviting, each man heard her call his name from her parted unkissed lips. Her neck was a slender V that led gracefully to the top of her thin frame. The men could not stop their eyes from continuing down to the gentle slopes of her waist, which was so tiny, it gave no indication of the shapely hips that followed.

She stood before them curiously, like a cat before a mouse, clasping
her hands together, and nodding to the first man to approach her.
Unwrapping the white-cotton scarf from his head, he walked forward
nervously, stumbling over himself. He looked up with the softest eyes,
smiling as best that a poor man could, hoping the wealth of his heart
was enough to win her hand. She told him, as she would tell every man:
If you wish for my hand, you must dissolve this great wall.

Without hesitation, he placed both hands upon its warm bricks, and pushed.
To his disappointment, the wall did not fall; in fact, it did not even sway.
With all his strength he tried again, but he slipped and fell to his knees.
Filled with sadness, he simply walked away without a word.

And so it went, one after another, they broke themselves against the wall.
Their tools could not penetrate it. Their ropes snapped. Their horses died.
Smiles faded upon the faithful who remained in the thinning line. Their
hearts were heavy with a defeat they had not yet experienced.
Suddenly, the high noon sun, floating through the blue above them
crashed into the wall, unable to pass. Pulled by western current,
the sun bobbed against the barrier, inching blindly around the
immovable barrier, eventually continuing into the afternoon.

Seeing this, all those remaining began their journey home,
walking silently past the Persian beauty and her great wall.
They slowly scattered out across the desert floor, looking down
into their broken hearts to see if there was anything left.
Occasionally, one would look back, for one last glimpse
of the beauty he traveled so far to claim, seeing only
her great wall towering over him in the distance.

Excuse me – startled, she spun around –
a charming young man stood confidently before her.
As she described the task before him, he smiled and
nodded that he understood her expectations, but his
eyes, full of wonder, weren't wishful like the others.
When she finished, he stepped toward the great wall
and kissed her tenderly, bringing himself so close
to her heart, she could no longer remember herself
without him. When she opened her eyes,
she could see nothing in the darkening landscape
except for her new love, whose face glowed
in the warm evening light of the horizon.

As she took his hand, she turned to find
the wall still standing before them.
After a moment to reflect, she smiled
and gazed adoringly into his eyes,

You're my true love, even if my wall still stands.
The man shook his head and released her hand.

Our kiss dissolved your expectations.
Your wall is gone. This wall is new.

Her eyes sprung open, filled with a sudden longing
for the impossible. As she breathed deeply, he watched her
slowly withdraw into herself. She stared past him,
like one overcome with blindness, looking for
the right words to express her heart's agony,
but could only manage a single question.
He responded, but all she heard was,

This wall is mine.

Halcyone. Hypnos. Morpheus

As the sun disappeared from her kingdom, she walked out onto her balcony
once more: the crowd erupted in joyous cheer as she waved goodnight.
Thousands of bachelors waited for the young widowed queen at the foot of the palace
gates. Some waited in open carriages with drivers and servants by their side,
while others stood barefoot with their arms full of red and yellow flowers;
all sought her hand in marriage the following morning.

Her entire kingdom called upon her to choose a suitor and complete the throne,
but with every suitor she saw, her eyes secretly grieved for her deceased husband
and her heart silently cried out to him, repeating his name over and again.
Rich with anxiety, she retired to her bed and laid down to rest
cradled between the short ivory horns of her bedposts.
Candlelight illuminated the silvery constellations engraved upon her ceiling

and she began counting

everything she had loved about her husband. She could not remarry unless
one could exceed all the qualities she missed of the deceased king. But as she counted
through the night, her list of attributes became so long she could no longer recall
all the qualities she desired in her husband. With great effort she tried to remember,
but her trembling lips could not hold the weight of their silence
and she bursts into tears, soaking her pillow with sadness.

Suddenly, an immense breath of air parted the balcony's silken drapes
and pulled upon the candle's dull flames, darkening her starry ceiling.
The candlelight soon regained its strength,

revealing the god of sleep, the conqueror of gods, the giver of peace,
standing in the enduring shadow of himself.
A golden headband held back his long black curls;
little wings fluttered beside his soft boyish face;
heavy eyelids concealed his sympathetic gaze.
She recognized the dark slender god before her,

but not the white-winged spirit that had carried him.
Candlelight penetrated the mists of his being, illuminating a thin ghostly frame.
A faint jaw, nose, and brow line completed the silhouette of his face.
Two cloudy orbs, swirling with consciousness, became fixed upon her;
Morpheus, the deity of dreams, saw before him eyes so alluring
that he *dreamed* of being dreamt through them. Her drowsy eyes could not endure

Hypnos' soft voice describing how loudly her heart cried out to be free;
for the entire night, in the deep silence of his palace, he could not sleep
from the pounding of the queen's heart, which he heard
as clearly as if his ear rested upon her breast. As he finally opened his sleepless eyes
His son Morpheus lifted him from his ebony couch and carried him,
as if out of a dream, into her bedroom to remedy her restless heart.

As one studies the starry night, his sleepy eyes studied her
thoughts, seeing at once, the great constellation of her lover
shining brightly in her memory. No mortal man could satisfy her
needs, for her heart knew just her husband's name. Only his son,
the god of dreams, could fulfill such perfection and give her heart rest,
for his formless spirit could take the shape of any man she desired.

When he spoke this message her eyes widened, revealing her heart,
in all its innocence, awakening in the arms of her husband, who smiled
at her surprise: his face was not pale with death, but glowed outwardly
as if in a meadow's summer light. She could feel the calluses of his hands
as he rubbed her arm and the gentle pulse in his fingertips
as he wiped away the tears from her eyes.

Off in the distance, she heard familiar voices calling out to her,
but before she could turn away from him, he pulled her closer
with a kiss softer than the breath of her sigh. From that moment on,
nothing could remove the immortalized smile on her face,
not even her servants, who shook their sleeping queen to no effect.

Heart-Shaped Box

Finally, one of the boys asked the young girl what was inside the heart-shaped box she carried with her. "Closterphopia," she replied. The boy snatched it from her hands and opened it, finding it empty. Puzzled, he closed it and handed it back to her. The box felt much lighter in her hands. As she looked down at it, her fingers toying with the lid's torn pink ribbon, a smile crept onto her face. They played together the rest of the afternoon.

The Mute Siren

(A Poem in 4 Parts)

I. Island of Psyche

In another lifetime,
the boy Zetetic was born blind and envious of all those that could see
the beloved women of his city Volupia, on the island of Psyche.
His entire youth was spent listening to the dramatic crooning of young men
publicly swooning over the beauty of the woman they beheld.
It was as if he sat alone in a theater of darkness, listening to actors
falling down upon the stage, announcing that their hearts had been struck
by the golden arrows of Eros, the god of love.
The public monologues were called "Love Songs"
and were sung in exactly the same way:

> *My Love! Oh, my Love! You are the rarest flower of all*
> *If Eros himself should see you, from heaven he would fall*
> *Your neck is a delicate stem holding your perfection*
> *The soft red petals of your cheeks are warm with affection*
> *My nose has found the sweet fragrance that hides within your hips*
> *My hand reaches for your ripened fruit with skin like soft lips*
> *But I dare not pluck or disturb the beauty that I dream*
> *Fearing I will awake to learn nothing is as it seems*
> *You, rarest flower of all, are neither fact nor fiction*
> *My Love! Oh, my Love! You're the rose of pure contradiction!*

After each performance he was unable to applaud, for he flung his eyes,
like two soft sponges, soaked in the dark waters of sadness,
into the familiar face of his hands.

He could hear the men run off his dark stage towards their new love.
How hard his eyes strained against the eternal darkness of his night,
trying to see the beauty that induced a song of love at first sight.
He could no longer bear to listen to those who sung
of a world where love was conceived in light,
for his world was almost all touch and sound:

Rooms were the creaks and echoes of movement;
The bath was the warm submersion of his feet;
The market was a great confusion of voices
and the clopping of horses along the street;
He walked upon the crunching of gravel
and slept upon the soft breath of his sheets.

Ill with loneliness, he sought the wisdom of the great oracle of Psyche, in the Temple of
Eros; the god of love, communicated to worshippers through this oracle.
But he knew not where the steps of the temple began.
So, he sought the guidance of his city's wisest philosopher, Charon, to guide him
with words.

II. The Philosopher's Words

As he ventured through the quiet town,
the warmth of day no longer pressed upon his cheeks
and a chill crept up from the empty street.

His unsteady steps filled the silence directly before him;
beside him were the muddled voices of those in their homes;
an impatient mother appeared in the darkness beside him,
loudly calling her son "Euthyphro" in for dinner.
A burning upward stride filled his legs and calves with fatigue.
The mother, still calling out to her child, was now far below him,
growing increasingly faint and distant.

His fist found itself upon a wooden door.
Each hard thud disappeared into the thick wood.
The door hinges squeaked.
Pork stew overwhelmed his nostrils.
A firm hand fell upon his shoulder;
Charon's voice greeted him,

Good evening Zetetic! Come in!

He entered the warmth of a stuffy unfamiliar room.
Aged woods and incense mixed with the steam of vinegar and salted pork.
Charon sat him down close to a bubbling pot of stew.
Touching the philosopher's hand, Zetetic said,

Dear Charon, I beg of you to tell me of the oracle of Psyche and how I should find it.
I should ask it, "When shall I sing my Love Song?"

Charon began:

> *Long ago the temple's golden pillars and vaulted roof were erected*
> *by the invisible servants of Eros, who instructed them to build it*
> *upon the most western cliff of this island,*
> *hidden by the pine-forests just beyond the city,*
> *the temple stands before the island's rocky cove, overlooking*
> > *the quiet waters of the Emerald Sea.*

It was there that he completed his union with Psyche,
the distant mother of our beautiful daughters.
But that first night, she quietly removed the veil of darkness
from her husband's face with the gentle light of her lamp, revealing
the most charming of the gods asleep. But when a drop of her lamp's burning oil
fell onto his shoulder, he surged forward from deep within himself
and opened his eyes. Startled by his awakening,
Pysche fell backwards, smashing her lamp upon the floor.

The invisible servant Philos quickly gathered the fire into his hands,
raised the glowing ball of light before them like a suspended star
illuminating the space between them. But Eros did not see this,
for his eyes were filled with sorrow; limbs heavy with disappointment.
He could only wonder what she hoped the lamp's light could reveal
that his love could not. With saddened eyes fixed upon his wife,
his white wings lifted him from the bed and carried him away
towards a pale moon. He continued to watch her
grow fainter in the distance until she was no more
than a memory.

Turning towards the suspended ball of flame,
she fell to her knees, clasped her hands together, and pleaded
as though in loud tearful prayer, for Philos' wisdom:
"Where can I find my true love?"

Zetetic, your heart asks the same question
and although the lamp that Psyche held has long since vanished,
its fire still burns in the invisible hand of Philos,
feeding only on the air around it.

Take the path that allows the sun rest
and leads you through miles of fresh pine scent.
When your horse refuses to take you further
you will have found the temple of Eros;
speak to the flame and you will receive an answer.

III. The Philosic Oracle

Rising the following morning, he navigated through his family's estate, exiting
into the warm darkness of his day, towards the shuffling of his hooves.
His horse stiffened as his hand found her dry spongy texture

                    of her face
              slope   and then down
          steep   the smooth
        up the   arch of her neck,
By sliding his hand

                              he calmed her large heart, and she relaxed.

Taking the leather reigns in his hand, he pulled himself onto her sturdy back
and with a gentle taping of his heals began his journey, leading his horse
away from the frantic voices of the market. The city soon disappeared
behind him as he entered the cool pine forest, which, like all forests, had no trees;
only a dark trackless path of snapping twigs.

He crossed it as he crossed all paths – be it beside a ravine or mountain pass – with
patience,
for there is no movement for him, only the rapid flutter of wings over his head,
or the unwelcomed touch of pine needles across his forehead. Except for these things,
he rocks atop his horse in isolation.

The heavy scent of pine fell further and further away from him.
Through wind-swept branches came the alluring scent of an orchard,
sweetened with spring blossoms and sun.

Light fluttered upon his face and leaves brushed past his arms.
Oranges ripened in his nostrils. Roses bloom beneath his feet.
He immediately felt the great depth of the sky above him
and heard the heavy splashing of a fountain in the open yard.

Dismounting the horse, he slowly passed through thin veils of mists
until the water's frigid lips met his. A cold current disappeared within him.

Walking carefully across the orchard's soft grass, he felt the warmth of day slowly recede from his legs, chest, and face. Hard granite steps appeared beneath his feet. He lunged up hard impenetrable blocks to the top.

The temple's breath flowed in and out of the open hall.
He felt the silent presence of pillars beside him and heard the shadow of each halted footstep upon the high vaulted ceilings above him.
Heat bloomed before his glaring eyes and a gentle voice addressed him.
He answered,

I am Zetetic. I seek the love that has eluded my eyes.
To find love is to find beauty, but beauty I have never beheld.
My eyes haven't adjusted to your eternal night; its darkness has become a blinding light.

Without hesitation, the oracle responded,

She awaits you atop a flowery islet in the middle of the emerald sea,
singing into the open sky for a lover who has yet to be. Her voice is so
enchanting and pure, it will pass into your heart like a lover's whisper.
Once touched by her beloved sound, no distance will remain, for you
will find yourself eternally beside her under the spell of her refrain.

IV. The Mute Siren

A distant melody emerged from the horizon.
The men clamored about on the ship, melting
down the sweet wax of honey and plugging their ears.
Movement soon ceased and Zetetic stood alone upon the deck of the ship,
slowly rocking in the wake of the oracle's prophecy.

The beautiful voice grew nearer, sweeping upward towards unseen clouds,
rippling through the gentle fabric of the sky, spreading into the heavens,
becoming lost in its own beautiful sorrow. The unending breath of her sigh
pressed upon his ears, restlessly pursuing his vulnerable heart.

Wave after wave of song poured over him, drowning him in wakeful dream:
through his unending veil of darkness appeared a tender feminine form.
Each note revealed the hidden curves and bendings of her body.
As her voice grew closer, her face emerged before him, as if from a shadow.
The tender sound of her lips and fluttering of her long blond hair. Suddenly,

he plunged into a great silence. The strange experience of her beauty vanished
in the swift up-rushing of salt water. When he surfaced, her song continued on
as did the ship with its sails flapping, folding, spreading in the sea-wind.

Following her voice, he swam into an obscure orchestra of sound:
Floating bones, trapped between rocks, resonated out from their cramped space;
hollowed boneheaps, piled upon the beach, whistled in the sea breeze.
Swimming ashore, he climbed the rocky embankment, crawled through the sweet
fragrance of the meadow, and sat before her, eyes wide open, transfixed, staring
blindly into her eyes, towards the last sound he heard, searching for beauty in the great
silence that now overcame her; seeing his adoring gaze, her heart was fulfilled,
and she no longer sighed.

His pale eyes beheld such boundless resolve for love
that he looked to be dreaming.
She could not hear his pleas for song,
nor understand the movement of his lips;
her eyes beheld a silent world:

At its center was Zetetic,
his pale eyes straining through each endless moment,
with a gaze so true that even after she had passed into eternal silence
death would not disturb him.

About the Author

John Everett Button is an American Poet and author of several other poetry collections, including the critically acclaimed epic poem *Reflexive Conversations*. A distinguished Philosophy graduate of East Carolina University, he holds an M.A. in Philosophy from Georgia State University. He currently lives in the Washington, DC area. Visit **www.JohnEverettButton.com** for more information.

Romantic Riddles

John Everett Button

www.ingramcontent.com/pod-product-compliance
Lightning Source LLC
Chambersburg PA
CBHW030759150426
42813CB00068B/3266/J